My Little Prayer Book

Mat 6:9 After this manner therefore pray ye: Our Father which art in heaven, Hallowed be thy name.

Mat 6:10 Thy kingdom come. Thy will be done in earth, as *it is* in heaven.

Mat 6:11 Give us this day our daily bread.

Mat 6:12 And forgive us our debts, as we forgive our debtors.

Mat 6:13 And lead us not into temptation, but deliver us from evil: For thine is the kingdom, and the power, and the glory, for ever. Amen.

This book is intended to help the reader in his or her daily talks with God.

ISBN-13:
978-0692427736
(*Home of the Barrd*)

ISBN-10:
0692427732

For more information, contact the Barrd

barrdofangels gmail.com

Morning Prayer

Blessed Heavenly Father
I thank Thee for this day
Help me, I beseech Thee
To walk within Thy way
Keep my soul, Oh Father
Safe from all alarm
And keep me safe, I beg Thee
From danger and from harm
As Thou hast sent Thy Spirit
To guard me in my sleep
Send Him this day to guide me
That I Thy Will may keep

Watch over all my labors, Lord
Help me to work as in Thy sight
That my yoke may be easy
And my burden light
Help me to follow my Savior
To be gentle, and tender, and mild
For I would that I may always
walk
As Thine Own beloved child
But, though I may fail in anything
Then, by Thy mercy and Thy
Word
Correct me and amend my fault
Through Jesus Christ our Lord
Amen

My Plea

My Lord, I believe
Help Thou my unbelief
Let my soul no longer grieve
Thy grace is my relief
Calm the raging sea of doubt
Bid the winds of wrath be still
Cast the wicked spirit out
You can heal me, if You will
Help the seed within me grow
Into a mighty tree
Your tender loving care bestow
This, Lord, is my plea
Amen

Song of Praise

God of the Universe,
Lord of creation
Prince of Peace,
And our Salvation,
Called "Wonderful!"
Called "Counselor!"
Called "The Mighty Conqueror!"
Beyond Space,
And beyond Time!
All Power and all Honor, Thine!
Who Was,
And Is,
And Is To Be,
All Praise and Glory unto Thee!
Amen

Amazing Grace

Oh, my Lord, I stand before Thee

Naked and ashamed

I have broken Thy commandment

I have sinned against Thy name

Forgive me, Lord, I beg Thee

Look not upon my sin

But look, instead, upon Thy Son

And let new life begin

Oh, my Father, I do thank Thee

For this Gift beyond all price

For Thine Own Beloved Son

My perfect Sacrifice

When I think He gave His life for me

In death He took my place
I am driven then to silence

By such Amazing Grace

Amen

Are You Calling Me?

Where are all the Christians, Lord?
Lord, where have they gone?
Whose minds were always on
Your word
Whose mouths were full of song?
Whose hands were busy at Your
work?
Whose heads were bowed in
prayer?
The world needs Your children,
Lord,
To show them You still care
Folks in sickness, folks in sorrow
They find it hard to cope
They need to feel Your loving
touch
They need Someone to give them
hope

They look up, but all they seem to
find
Is an empty sky above
They need to know that Someone
cares
They need to feel Your love
There are people, Lord, so lonely
They need a loving friend
Where are all the Christians, Lord?
Is there no one You can send?
There are people, Lord, who are
lost
Where can your children be
Is there no one, Lord, to hear
Your call?

Lord?

Are You calling me?
Amen

Faith

Tossed upon my mind's oceans
Burning with my deepest emotions
Ridden with my guilts and fears
Watered with my bitter tears
Teaching me trust in a world of deceit
Teaching me to be gentle and meek
Showing me love in world filled with
hate
Showing me grace that has opened the
gate
Building on my heart's tenderness
Filling me with wild happiness
Oh, with what joy my soul has received!
I know in Whom I have believed.
Amen

Dialogue With The Deity

"My Lord, I am foolish
And far from being wise"
"I will give you wisdom, child,
And open up your eyes"
1 Cor 1:30

"I feel so all alone, my Lord,
Without a single friend."
"I will be with you always
Even until the end."
Matt 28:20

"My Lord, I can't do anything!
My strengths are far too few."
"You can do all things, My child,
For I will strengthen you."
Phil 4:13

"I am so very tired, my Lord.
I cannot give my best."
"Come unto Me, My precious child,
And I will give you rest"
Matt 11:28-30
"

I feel so insufficient, Lord,
I just can not go on."
My grace is sufficient, child,
And I will lead you home."
2 Cor 12:9

I am so afraid, my Lord!
The enemy is near!"
"I have sent My Spirit, child
That you should have no fear."
2 Tim 1:7

"My worries are so many, Lord,
I don't know what to do."
"Cast your cares upon Me, child,
For I care for you."
1 Pet 5:7

"My Lord, I just can't manage.
I can not make ends meet."
"My precious child, trust in Me,
And I'll supply all your needs."
Phil 4:19

"No one really loves me, Lord,
"My friends have not been true"
"I love you so, My precious child
I gave Myself for you."
John 3:16

"I'm lost in the darkness, Lord,
My way I can not see."
"I'll direct your steps, My child,
If you'll just hold on to Me.
Prov 20:24

"The evil I have done, Lord,
I just can not forgive!"
"My child, I have forgiven you.
Come unto Me, and live."
1 John 1:9, Rom 8:1

"Oh, Lord, its just impossible:
Such love just can not be!"
"Oh, My precious, precious child,
All is possible with Me"
Luke 18:27

For Thy Comforter

When I look at the world around me
All the violence and all the hate
I wonder "Where is the Savior's love"?
And "Where is Heaven's Gate"?
It's so hard to hold on to faith
When all that I can see
Are the hordes of Satan's army
Whose battle cry is "me, me, me!"
Oh, God, it so often seems
That faith is just pretension
And there is no one who believes
In Your Holy intervention
Oh Father, look down at the world
Can't You hear the people crying?
Can't You see how much we need You
now
Can't You see that love is dying?
Oh, Lord, send to us Thy Comforter
That we may know that You still care
Send Thy Spirit to revive our faith
This, Lord, is our prayer
Amen

For Simple Blessings

Dear Father, we do thank You
For the blessings You have given
Of food and rest and comfort here
And a place with You in Heaven
Amen

Direct My Steps

Your voice, Oh Blessed Father
Seems so very hard to hear
Although I sense Your Holy
Presence
I know, somehow, that You are
near
Dear Father, please direct my steps
Please help me, Lord, to know
The road that You would have me
take
The direction I should go
Where is the task You have for
me?
Amen

Lord Deliver Me

My Father, I fear my enemy

I fear his deadly power
Roaring like a raging lion
Seeking whom he might devour
From his deceit and tyranny
Lord, keep me safe, I pray
For he lies in wait for me
Claws unsheathed to slay

For he knows the evil of my heart
And just what snares to set
He knows just where to aim each
dart
Just how to spread his net

†

Oh, lead me not into temptation
But deliver me this day
My Father, guard me through the
night
And keep me in Thy way
Amen

For Christian Unity

Be with us, Lord, we humbly pray
In all that we may do or say
That we may tell thy loving grace
And spread Thy love to every place
Help us to know that we are one
In the heart of Thy Beloved Son
Amen

Faith

Dilemma

I don't know just what to think
Sometimes I get so awfully mixed
up
There are problems everywhere I
look
Why doesn't God just get it all
fixed up
The bills are all just piling up
There's a mortgage on my house
My kids are mean and ungrateful
And I have a cheating spouse
And yet you say God loves me
What could you be saying
Everywhere around me
I see my world decaying

Lord, my faith is sorely tested
I'm hemmed in on every side
Help me Lord, to find Your peace
Help my love, Lord, to abide
Lord, there's chaos all around me
Even in my dreams
Help me to put my trust in You
No matter how hard it seems
Oh Jesus, won't you hurry up
Bring an end to this sad story
And bring Your children, Lord, at
last
To dwell with You in Glory
Amen

Even Me Lord?

"For all have sinned and
fallen short of God's Glory"
This is Mankind's
sad, sad story
Who could all these
"sinners" be?
Even me, Lord? Even me?
But God made a Promise,
He gave His Word
He would send His Son
to save the world
Who would the Anointed One
set free?
Even me, Lord? Even me?
He said, "I have come
to seek and find
And not one
shall be left behind.
They will be in
Paradise with Me."

Even me, Lord? Even me?
For the price of sin,
the Messiah died
The Lamb of God
was crucified
For whom did He
hang upon that tree?
Even me, Lord? Even me?
"I will write My Name
upon your hearts.
By faith, I will help you to make a
new start.
Yes, I will come and dwell with
thee."
Even me, Lord? Even me?
"Now, look:
I will send you forth
To be My witness
in all the earth.
You will teach others

to hear and to see."
Even me, Lord? Even me?
"I will be your
Loving Friend
I'll stay with you always,
until the end
I'll give everlasting
life to thee."
Even me, Lord? Even me?
"And now,
before My Judgment Seat
I'll reward each one,
as is meet
With the Glory My Father
has given to Me."
Even me, Lord? Even me?
Amen

Consecrated Lord to Thee

In the comforting Presence
of my King
Unafraid of what the world may
bring
Sealed by His Spirit, bought with
His Love
And guarded by angels sent from
above
Gently led through the paths of life
Guided through every pain and
strife
Like a kitten in her Master's lap
Curled up for a cozy nap
Gazing up into His Beloved Face
Secure within His Loving Grace
This is what it is to be
Consecrated, Lord, to Thee!
Amen

Look Up

Alone upon my bed I cry!
Can it all have been a lie?
Will God hear me, now, today?
Is there any use to pray?
Could the Lord have forgotten the Word
He has spoken?
Is our Faith all for nothing, His
promises broken?
Where is God in this world?
The Evil One's banners are all unfurl'd!
Hatred runs rampant out in the street!
The children are crying for something
to eat!
Abuse and violence are the rules,
While God's people seem like fools.
Love has grown dirty, and marriage a
sham!
Where, oh where is the Great "I AM"?
We are losing our young ones to
"gangs" and to "drugs".
Their "heroes" are "punks" and
"gangsters" and "thugs".

New diseases every day!
Has the Healer gone away?
We pollute the ground, the sea, the sky.
Has God left us all to die?
Listen to the people weeping!
Is God dead? Or is He sleeping?
Babies are ripped from their mother's
womb!
Their sanctuary has become their tomb.
Fathers want freedom! Mothers want
choice!!
But listen!! There's a Still Small
Voice...
God is saying, "I still care
Be still, My Children, do not despair.
Look up! Your salvation is drawing
near!
The Conqueror comes! So do not fear."

A Simple Prayer

Lord, I would follow Thee!
Wherever You may go
Open my eyes,
that I may see
My heart, that I may know
Lord, I would follow Thee
This is all my prayer
I would Thy disciple be
And know Thy loving care
Amen

Teach Me Lord

Teach me Lord, and guide my way

I love You more each passing day.

Guide me Lord, You are my heart

To me Your love You do impart

When it is difficult to cope

You are my strength, You are my hope.

You help me up if I should fall

You are my guide, You are my all

Teach me Lord, and guide my way

I love You more each passing day

Amen

Prayer for Home and Family

Shed, oh Lord, thy Shining Light

Upon this household, day and night

Help us, Lord, to love each other

Father, Mother, Sister, Brother

Guide us, Lord, along our way

As we go about our tasks each
day

Create in us a gallant heart

Watch over us when we must part

Be with us through every stress

Help us, Lord, to pass the test

When it is difficult to cope

Be our ever present hope

Let our courage never fail

As we weather every gale

Help us to tell Thy wondrous story

And bring us, at last, unto Thy
glory

All this, according to Thy word

We ask through Jesus Christ Our
Lord

Amen

The Lord's Prayer

Father in Heaven, we praise Thee
Thy Blessed Will be done
Peace on earth, and Thy goodwill
To each and every one
Give us this day our daily bread
Fulfill, Lord, every need
As on Thy Holy Mountain,
The Lamb and the Lion feed
Forgive us, Lord, we beg Thee
Every jealousy, greed, and lust
And help us to forgive all those
Who trespass against us
Lead us not into temptation
Guard us from evil, Lord
For Thine is the Kingdom and
Glory
According to Thy Word
Amen

The Saint's Prayer

(based on the prayer by St. Francis of Assisi)

Be thou, Oh Father, ever with me
And let Thy peace be seen in me
Where there is hatred, let me sow
Thy love
Where doubt, faith in the Lord
above
Where despair, let me teach hope
in Thee
Thy pardon for every injury
Where there is darkness, let me
shine Thy light
And where there is sadness, Thy
joy so bright

Not to be consoled, but to console
This is Thy plan to make me
whole
Let me be Thy example, Lord
Let me bring Thy love to a hate-
filled world
Not to be understood, but to
understand
In Thee, Oh Lord, have I made
my stand
For it is in giving that we receive
As Thou hast taught us to believe
To Thee, Oh Lord, my life I give
For it is in dying that I live
Amen

The Writer's Prayer

Oh, Lord, I'm just a woman

Created by Thy hand

Full of human emotions

I don't always understand

You have given unto me

A voice, and I must write

Words are the substance of my life

My joy and my delight

My pen speaks of love and
laughter

My pen may speak of sorrow

Or tell of shining yesterdays

Or peer into tomorrow

My pen may speak of feelings

Of lies spoken, trust betrayed

Oh, Lord, how it saddens me

When these slip unto the page

Lord please guide my fingers

As I put them to this task

Let my pen speak only peace

Oh, Lord, I humbly ask

Let me speak of mercy

Let me speak of love

Let me tell of a risen Savior

And a home with Thee, above

Amen

The Warrior's Prayer

Heavenly Father, hear us now

As humbly we our heads do bow

Strike off the scales from our eyes

That we may see through Satan's
lies

Give us ears that we may hear

And know the enemy is near

Give us patience, Lord, we pray

As we march into the fray

Give us grace, Lord, to forgive

For in You our lives we live

Give us wisdom, that we might reach

Broken hearts, Thy love to teach

Let Thy mercy be our Sword

Our shield be Thy Holy Word

When the heathen rage, Thou wilt defend

Lord, be with us until the end

Amen

God Bless America

Oh, what has happened to this
land
Where all was well, and life was
good
In God we trust...United we stand
And children were safe in the
neighborhood?

Where "parents" meant a Dad and
Mother
And folks put their faith in God
Now, we have a "significant other"
And innocence seems odd

We asked God to leave our
classrooms
From the courthouse, He was sent
We said "We do not need You"
And sadly then, He went

Oh, our precious Land of the Free
And sweet Home of the Brave
Oh, why can't you hear, why don't
you see?
You'd better wake up before it's
too late!

Once proud leader among the
nations
Can't you see how you are falling?
Others now will hold your station
The situation is appalling

Oh, people, get down on your knees
And for your country, pray
Precious Father, won't You please
Come back to us today!

Amen

My Offering

God Who was made flesh for me

Nailed upon a lonely tree

What gift could I bring

That would suffice

To repay such great sacrifice

All that I am I lay at Your throne

Make me, Lord, Your very Own

Amen

Freedom

(a series of Japanese Haiku)

Lord, You call me friend

when my place is at Your feet

truly I am blessed

You call me Your child

though You made me of the dust

surely You love me

You give me Your peace

though a sinner I have been

truly this is grace

You give me new Life

though I was destined to die

Yours I am always

You hung on the tree

blood and mercy flowing down

from Your wounded side

You have paid my price

You gave Your own life for me

the Son set me Free

Amen

Holy Fire

Dear Father, Thou Almighty One
Great in Mercy and in Grace
Send us Thy Spirit, Lord we pray
Be with us here, within this place
Kindle within us the fire of love
Make us pure with cleansing flame
Purge us, Lord, of all our sins
And take away our shame
Make us worthy, Lord, to worship
Thee
As Thou hast taught us in Thy
Word
With humble hearts, in spirit and
truth
Through Jesus Christ, our Lord
Amen

Evening Prayer

Blessed Heavenly Father
Grant me peace, I pray
Keep me safe under Thy wing
At the close of day
With this day's accomplishments
Contented I will be
Help me to forgive my enemies
As Thou hast forgiven me
Now in Thy Holy Comfort
As I close my eyes
I look to Thee, my Father
As evening fills the skies
Bless all those who love me
Bless those who hate me, too
And bring me, Lord, at close of
day
Closer, ever closer to You
Amen

May the Lord
look down upon you
and bless you
in all your ways.
Amen

Deborah Anne Bard